First published in Great Britain by
Pendulum Gallery Press
56 Ackender Road, Alton, Hants GU34 1JS

© TONI GOFFE 1990

HAPPY? RETIREMENT
ISBN 0-948912-10-3

PRINTED IN GREAT BRITAIN BY
UNWIN BROTHERS LTD, OLD WOKING, SURREY

"I WAS JUST GOING TO GIVE HIM ONE, WHEN HE SUDDENLY, ROLLED OVER AND DIED WITH THAT SMILE ON HIS FACE!"

"OH BOY, ROLL ON RETIREMENT, SO I CAN GET ME ONE OF THOSE...."

"....AND WE'VE ALL PUT TOGETHER FOR A
    LITTLE LEAVING PRESENT FOR YOU ALICE"

"THANK YOU FOR GIVING US 45 YEARS OF YOUR LIFE AT THIS OFFICE, — WE'VE CLUBBED TOGETHER TO PRESENT YOU WITH THIS....."

"A RETIREMENT KISSAGRAM DOES NOT CONSTITUTE SEXUAL HARASSMENT M^s MARPLE ......"

" SIR, NEGATIVE, ON THE M^S MARPLE -RETIREMENT -
-KISSAGRAM ......"

" YES, GEORGE I KNOW YOU RETIRE TODAY,...
.........BUT!, NOT TILL 5·30 PM. "

"THANK YOU FOR TAKING EARLY RETIREMENT, GEORGE, MEET YOUR REPLACEMENT, TRACY!"

"WELL GEORGE, YOUR LAST DAY!! IS THERE ANYTHING YOU'D LIKE TO DO BEFORE YOU GO?..."

"OF COURSE IT'S ALRIGHT TRACY, THINK OF IT AS MY RETIREMENT PRESENT....."

" OFFICE PARTIES WON'T BE THE
SAME WITHOUT YOU, Mr SMYTHE ....."

" ...AND FOR YOUR RETIREMENT PRESENT FOR 50 YEARS OF HARD WORK FOR US....A SET OF GARDENING TOOLS......

"WHAT TIME'S DINNER? OH I'M NOT DOING THAT ANY MORE ———— I'VE RETIRED TOO!!"

"YOU'RE LETTING YOURSELF GO SINCE YOU RETIRED — AND THAT'S ONLY **TWO-HOURS** AGO!!"

"WHAT ARE YOU DOING BACK HERE GEORGE, THIS IS YOUR SEVENTH VISIT AND YOU RETIRED ONLY A WEEK AGO!"

"YOU KNOW WHAT MATILDA, THEY'RE HAVING THEIR FIRST TEA-BREAK AT THE OFFICE, ABOUT NOW...."

"Oi! WHERE ARE YOU GOING?? YOU'RE RETIRED!!"

" LATE FOR WORK AGAIN, EH, GODFREY ? "

" HELLO GEORGE, I THOUGHT YOU'D RETIRED.!?"

"I CAN'T UNDERSTAND HOW THEY'VE KEPT GOING WITHOUT ME......"

" IS THIS ALL ?? WHAT ABOUT
MY EXPENCES ?? "

" I WISH I COULD AFFORD TO RETIRE.
LIKE YOU ARTHUR ...."

"SITTING ON THE COUCH ALL WEEKEND WITH YOUR LEGS CROSSED IS NOT MEDITATING!!"

"RETIREMENT? OH IT'S JUST PUSHING THE VACUUM-
- CLEANER AROUND ONE MORE EXTRA OBJECT......"

"DON'T BE FUNNY ARTHUR, JUST LIFT YOUR FEET!"

"TV? NO, THAT'S FOR WASHING CLOTHES..."

"I'LL BE GLAD WHEN I'VE HAD ENOUGH OF THIS PROGRAMME....."

"IF YOU'RE GOING TO SIT THERE ALL DAY, WHY DON'T
YOU JUST WATCH THE GOLDFISH, IT WOULD SAVE
ELECTRICITY..."

" THIS IS SO BAD, I JUST CAN'T TURN
IT OFF "

" WAKE UP DEAR, YOUR T.V. BANQUET IS ARRIVING.."

"ANOTHER EVENING OF T.V., FALLING ASLEEP AND WISHING I'D DONE SOMETHING ELSE— BUT WHAT?"

" WHEN I SAY I'M STIFF, I MEANT <u>MY BACK!</u> "

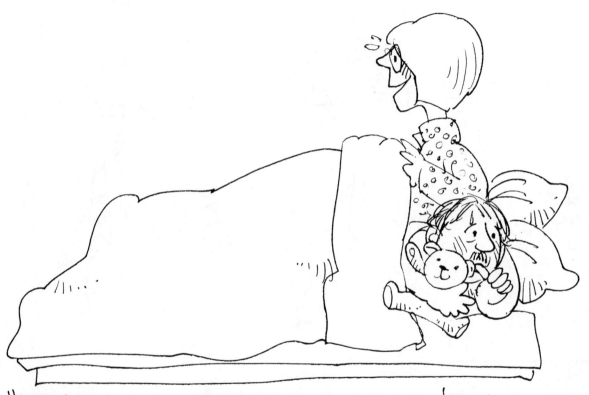

"THAT WAS GREAT, YOU HAVEN'T FORGOTTEN A THING..."

"I'M NOT GETTING TIRED OF SEX WITH YOU DEAR, IT'S JUST THAT, I SEEM TO LOOKFORWARD MORE AND MORE TO THE TEA AFTERWARDS ...."

" WAKE UP! TIME FOR SOME BEDROOM
FUN AND GAMES!... "

"WHAT TIME IS IT?! TIME WE HAD SOME MORE FUN AROUND HERE....."

" YOU DIDN'T FORGET TO TAKE FIDO FOR HIS WALK AGAIN, DID YOU ?? "

"WHEN YOU RETIRED, HOW MUCH OF YOU STOPPED WORKING?"

"WHAT YOU NEED IS A NICE HOBBY, LIKE **HOUSEWORK!!** "

"I CAN'T MOVE MY FEET, I'VE GOT A PUSSY ON MY LAP!"

" WHAT AM I DOING ? <u>THIS</u>!! <u>THIS</u>! IS WHAT I'm DOING <u>THIS</u>!! " .

" WILL YOU STOP MOPING ABOUT THE HOUSE,
— GO OUTSIDE AND MOPE .... "

"CAN I COME AND MOPE IN YOUR HOUSE MABEL,
I'VE BEEN THROWN OUT OF MINE...."

"GEORGE, I'M GETTING FED UP WITH YOU HANGING AROUND THE HOUSE"

"I CAN'T STAND HIM HANGING AROUND THE HOUSE, I'VE HAD TO GO OUT AND GET A JOB!"

"TAKE NO NOTICE, HE'S JUST CONTEMPLATING HIS LOST YEARS...."

"HE'S BEEN DEEPLY DISTURBED, SINCE HIS RETIREMENT!"

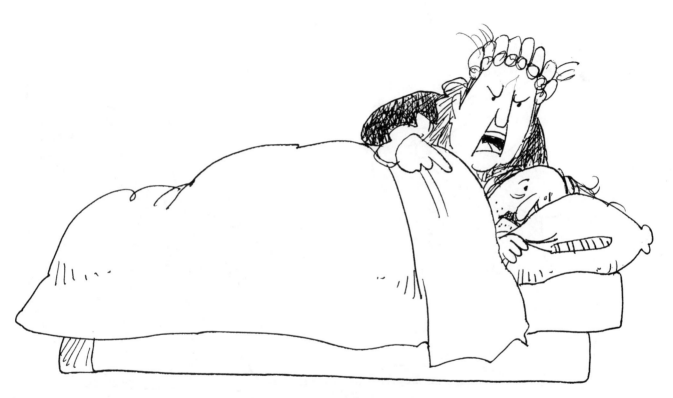

"YOU AND YOUR URGES, THE ONLY URGES YOU GET IS THE URGE TO TURN OVER AND GO TO SLEEP!"

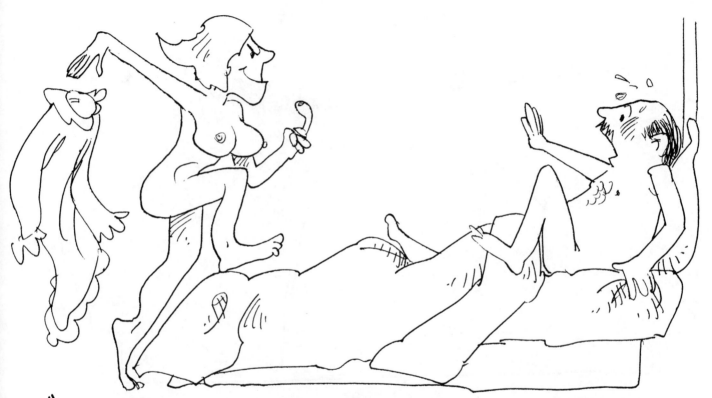

"JUST BECAUSE I'M HOME ALL DAY, DOESN'T MEAN WE'VE GOT TO DO IT EVERY DAY! JULIE!

" RETIRED! YOU SHOULD BE RETYRED,
YOUR TREAD IS WEARING OUT....."

"NOW, AFTER ALL THOSE YEARS OF WORK......
.... TIME TO RELAX."

"WHAT TIME DOES THE TEA-TROLLY COME AROUND?"

" THE SECRET IS TO CARRY A SHOVEL
AROUND WHERE EVER YOU GO - KEEPS THEM
OFF YOUR BACK ..."

"THEY'RE FOR MY NEW HOBBY I'M STARTING IN THE GARDEN SHED — MINIATURE GARDENS!! "

"LET'S DRINK TO 'GARDEN SHEDS'...."

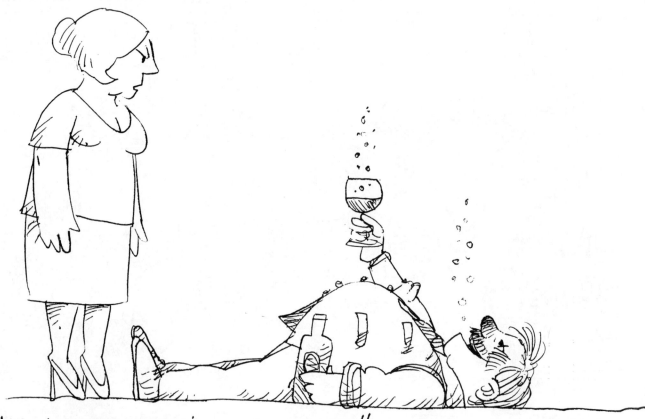

"THIS WINE-MAKING IS GREAT!! SARAH, WHY DON'T YOU GET UP OFF THE FLOOR AND TRY SOME??"

"I'M MORE BUSY SINCE I RETIRED, THAN I EVER WAS AT WORK!"

"I WISH I COULD REMEMBER WHAT THEY CALL THAT, WHAT THEY'RE DOING....."

" WELL AT LEAST YOUR DOG'S ENJOYING YOUR
RETIREMENT GEORGE ....."

" WILL YOU *CUT THAT OUT* !! "

"SHE WANTED ME TO HAVE A HOBBY, BUT I DON'T HAVE TIME, WHAT WITH WALKING THE DOG....."

"WHEN I SUGGESTED MUSIC AS A HOBBY, I HAD SOMETHING MORE SEDATE IN MIND!"

"NOW, WHAT DO I DO?"

"I HOPE YOU'RE WASHING DOWN THE WALLS FIRST, DEAR!"

"LOOK DEAR, MY FIRST OMELETTE..."

"I DON'T THINK WE DO SEX, AS A HOBBY, HERE SIR ..."

" ....AND HOW ARE YOU ENJOYING YOUR RETIREMENT MR JONES...."

"GROUP SEX SOUNDS FUN, BUT HOW DO WE START..?"

"MARRIED?, OF COURSE WE'RE MARRIED!!
DON'T WE LOOK MARRIED??"

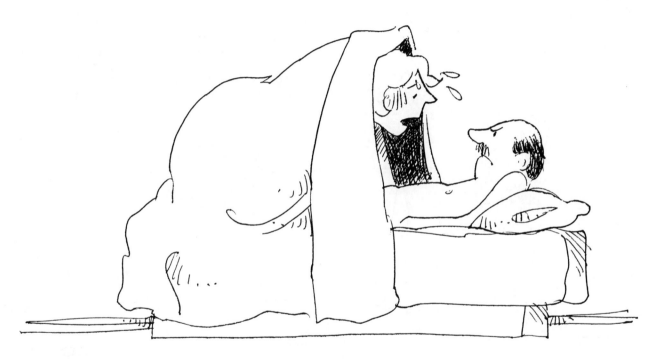

"WELL, IF I CAN'T FIND IT AFTER HALF AN HOUR, HOW LONG DO YOU WANT ME TO GO ON LOOKING?"

"OH, COMPUTERS! I USED TO DO THAT, EVERY DAY TO LONDON AND BACK FOR 40 YEARS.."

" GRANDAD, IS THERE SEX AFTER RETIREMENT?! "

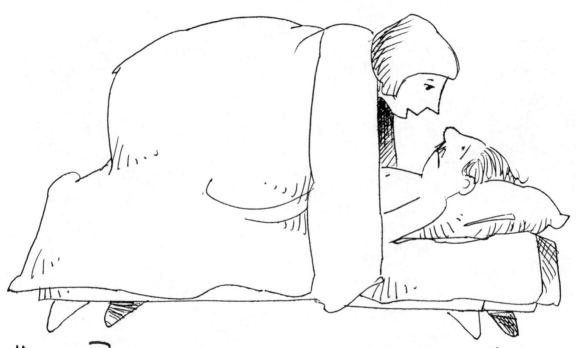

" WHAT DO YOU THINK THE DOG IS LAUGHING AT?... "

" HAVE YOU FED THE ANIMALS TODAY ? "

"DON'T MOVE M'DEAR, I'VE GOT A SUPRISE FOR YOU..."

" WOW, ALL THOSE STAIRS, YOU'D BETTER START WITHOUT ME ....."

"A YOUNG LADY TO SEE YOU GEORGE, SOMETHING ABOUT YOU SAYING GOODBYE AT YOUR RETIREMENT PARTY.......
.... NINE MONTHS AGO!!

" I TRIED D.I.Y, BUT, FOUND I COULDN'T REACH....."

'WELL, MUST GO BACK TO THE LITTLE WOMAN...
....THEN HOME TO THE WIFE!'

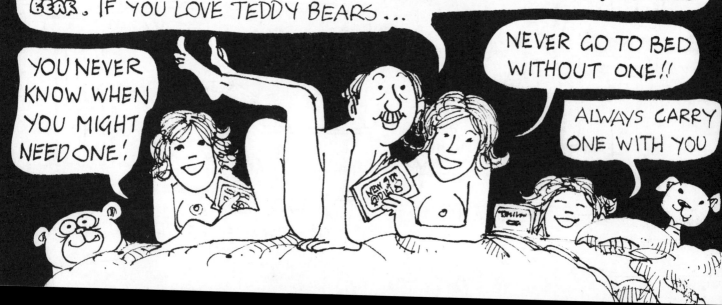